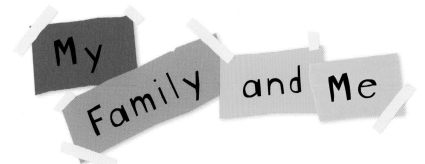

My Family and Me

Welcoming a New Baby

Mary Auld

FRANKLIN WATTS
LONDON•SYDNEY

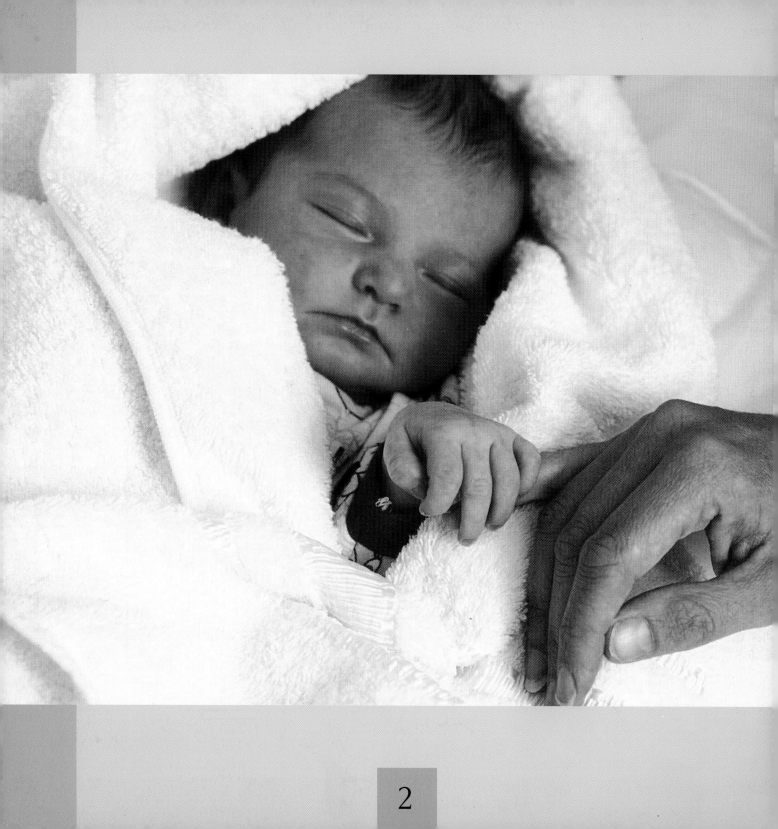

It is a very special time when a new baby is born. It is the start of a new life.

? Your turn...

What day were you born on? How long have you been alive?

A baby grows inside its mum's tummy for nine months before it is born. The whole family gets ready for the baby's arrival.

" Zoe says...

"I used to talk to my baby brother inside my mum's tummy – although I didn't know he was a boy then!"

Most babies are born in
hospital. Families often go
to visit them there.

Billy and Olive took presents for their mum and the new baby.

? Your turn...
What present would you give a new baby?

Some babies are born early and are too small to go home for a while. Their mum helps to look after them in hospital.

Marco says...
"I was born early. My mum spent all the time she could with me until I was strong enough to go home."

It's exciting bringing a new baby home.

Ed and his family made his new sister's room just right.

Maria's granny came to stay for a few days to help out.

Your turn...

Who helped to look after you when you were a baby?

Everyone in the family is busy with a new baby around.

Raj and Anita help to feed their brother.

Leo helps his dad change his baby sister's nappy.

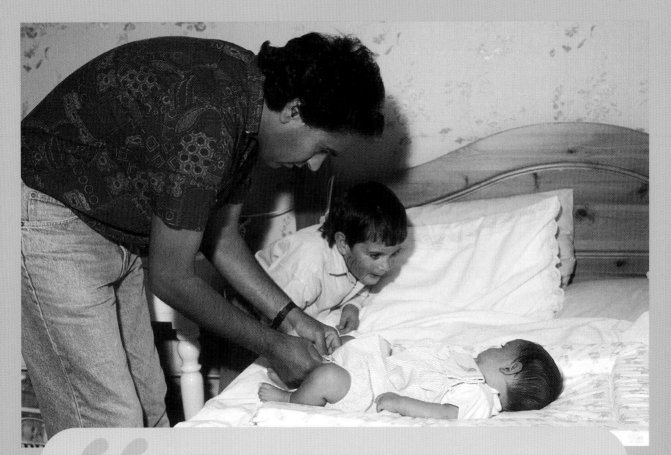

Leo says...
"I try to make Rosie laugh while Dad puts her clothes back on."

Everyone likes to kiss and cuddle a baby to say hello.

When Paul's parents first adopted him, they held him all the time.

Emma likes to cuddle up on the sofa with her family.

? Your turn...
Have you ever held a baby?
What did it feel like?

Many people have special
ceremonies to name a baby.
Sky's parents planted a tree at
her naming ceremony.

Daniel was named at a christening. Everyone welcomed him into the Christian religion.

" Daniel's brother says...
"He was good and didn't cry, even when the priest put water on his head."

There are lots of other special ceremonies to welcome a new baby. Rajinder's family bounced him in sweets during the Sikh festival of Lohi.

? Your turn...
Did your family have a special ceremony to welcome you?

18

Babies grow up quickly. We celebrate the day we were born every year - on our birthday.

66 Neil says...

"On my birthday, Grandad always says he remembers me when **I** was no bigger than a flea!"

How would you
welcome a new baby
to your family?

Some things to do

Ask your parents what you were like when you were a baby. What do they remember about the first time you came home?

With your friends, make a collection of photos of you all as babies. Can you recognise who is who?

Make a list of all the different things you can think of that you need to do to look after a baby.

Write a poem or tell a story about the birth of a new baby.

About this book

The aim of this book is to give children the opportunity to explore what their family means to them and their role within it in a positive and celebratory way. In particular it emphasises the importance of care and support within the family. It also encourages children to compare their own experiences with other people, recognising similarities and differences and respecting these as part of daily life.

Children will get pleasure out of looking at this book on their own. However, sharing the book on a one-to-one basis or within a group will also be very rewarding. Just talking about the main text and pictures is a good starting point, while the panels also prompt discussion:
• Question panels ask children to talk directly about their own experiences and feelings.
• Quote panels encourage them to think further by comparing their experiences with those of other children.

First published in 2007 by
Franklin Watts, 338 Euston Road
London NW1 3BH

Franklin Watts Australia
Level 17/207 Kent Street
Sydney NSW 2000

Copyright © Franklin Watts 2007
A CIP catalogue record for this book is available from the British Library.
Dewey classification: 305.232

ISBN: 978 0 7496 7627 8

Series editor: Rachel Cooke
Art director: Jonathan Hair
Design: Jason Anscomb

Picture credits: Paul Baldesare/Photofusion: 20. John Birdsall/John Birdsall Photo Library: 5, 8, 14, 15. Tim Dub/Photofusion: Cover, 2. Laura Dwight/Corbis: 11. ER Productions/Corbis: 6. Sally Greenhill/Sally & Richard Greenhill: 7, 12, 17. Judy Harrison/Photofusion: 13, 19. Hannah Marsh/John Birdsall Photo Library: 24. Chuck Savage/Corbis: 10. Mo Wilson/Photofusion:16. Every attempt has been made to clear copyright. Should there be any inadvertent omission please apply to the publisher for rectification.

Please note that some of the pictures in this book have been posed by models.

Printed in China

Franklin Watts is a division of Hachette Children's Books.